QUILLING PATTERNS

FOR BEGINNERS

A Complete Guide to Quickly Learn Paper Quilling Techniques with Illustrated Pattern Designs to Create All Your Project Ideas

by Brenda Sanders

All trademarks inside this book are for clarifying purposes only and are possessed by the owners themselves, not allied with this document.

Disclaimer

All erudition supplied in this book is specified for educational and academic purpose only. The author is not in any way to be responsible for any outcomes that emerge from using this book. Constructive efforts have been made to render information that is both precise and effective, but the author is not to be held answerable for the accuracy or use/misuse of this information.

Foreword

I will like to thank you for taking the very first step of trusting me and deciding to purchase/read this life-transforming book. Thanks for investing your time and resources on this product.

I can assure you of precise outcomes if you will diligently follow the specific blueprint I lay bare in the information handbook you are currently checking out. It has transformed lives, and I firmly believe it will equally change your own life too.

All the information I provided in this Do It Yourself piece is easy to absorb and practice.

Table of Contents

INTRODUCTION

Paper quilling is the art of rolling, shaping, gluing and embellishing strips of paper. This method is also called paper filigree or merely quilling. You need a tool called a quill to produce the standard coiled shape of the paper. You then glue the paper at the top and shape the coils to form numerous designs, such as flowers, leaves and other various decorative designs.

This ornamental technique of using paper goes back to the Renaissance, when nuns used the coiled paper designs to decorate book covers, bookmarks and spiritual items. At this time the most frequently used type of paper was the gilded edges of the pages of books. The nuns coiled the little strips of these gilded edges to imitate the iron latticework of the period. It was an art practiced by mostly women in the 18th century and was one of the techniques that young girls needed to discover as part of their studies. The colonists brought the art with them when they emigrated to America. The majority of the quilled paper designs that have actually been secured are of spiritual artwork.

The art of quilling did die out for a time, but has just recently become a very popular craft. This is because of the low cost of the paper materials needed to make designs to embellish boxes and invitations and especially pages of scrapbooks, with the increased interest in scrapbooking.

The tools you need to get going in quilling are very fundamental, such as; strips of paper, something to wind the strips around and glue. The strips of paper can be cut in widths of 1/8 inch to I inch, but the majority of people use 1/8 inch strips. You can select the paper in whatever weight you desire, however the standard is construction paper, which can be found in a range of colors. The winding tool can be a toothpick or a needle, but you can likewise check out a craft shop to buy a specifically created quill.

Other tools that you require include sharp scissors for cutting the paper and a ruler to make sure that you cut all the strips the very same size. You can cover a piece of corrugated cardboard with wax paper, instead of using the top of a table, This will keep the glue from getting onto the table. You need to also have a moist fabric at hand for cleaning the glue off your fingers.

A few of the simple designs you can start out with include:

- A V-shape style includes folding the strip of paper in half and rolling the ends of the outside of the paper around the quill. You have to roll the paper far from the inner crease.

- Feelers include rolling just part of the strip of paper. You can get this design by folding the strip in half or by using an in-folded strip.

- Coiling the paper either loosely or very securely around the quill can give a peacock eye.

Using quilling varies from decorating photos that can be framed and hung, to celebration cards, from picture frames to 3 dimensional objects. Flower designs are often a favorite for a lot of quillers, but animals, scenes, landscapes and balanced patterns are all highly effective. The very nature of the art of quilling gives it a more three dimensional designs and adds new possibilities to pictures.

There are many ways for coiling your paper; French and Italian nuns used to use goose quills for this reason. You can use a needle or a toothpick, however it is better to buy a specially developed slotted quilling tool, these are relatively affordable and very effective. You can use any kind of white glue as long as it dries clear.

The great feature of the art of quilling is that it appropriates for all levels of capability. You can rapidly discover how to make easy styles and fundamental shapes, but more advanced quillers can make highly intricate, ornate and delicate designs. Some quillersspecialise in three dimensional designs.

Imagine sitting at your kitchen table. In front of you are some narrow strips of colored paper; a tool that looks like a hat pin, and a little bottle of craft glue.

Paper quilling is a craft that invites newbies with open arms. All it takes is to learn every fundamental strategy, from rolling various shapes to scrolling, fringing, looping, and weaving paper.

Soon, you'll be displaying your custom-made quillwork with pride, making unique quilled gifts for family and friends, and sharing new methods and concepts with other paper filigree crafters.

CHAPTER ONE

Basics Of Quilling Paper

Quilling can be an enjoyable art and it can be an excellent way to enliven your scrapbooks, customize your gifts, and make your handmade cards remarkable and special. Quilling undoubtedly is an easy method to reveal your creativity. For sure you would love quilling if you like paper crafting and making designs on your own.

Quilling has long been used in cardmaking. Now we know the paper is wound around a piece of quill to produce the basic coil. These coils are used to form various ornaments and patterns that are similar to pattern work.

The Renaissance period had seen French and Italian nuns and monks who are using quilling in decorating cards, covers of books and religious items. During those times, they use paper strips that were trimmed from edges of books. These strips were rolled in order to produce the quill shapes.

During the 18th century, this particular technique in cardmaking became popular among the groups of elite ladies. It was included in the list of one of the things that they can do without getting tired, physically or mentally.

Further, the Americas had also seen quilling spread across the continent, and used not only in cardmaking but in other forms as well. Many artworks can be seen on stands, cabinets, cribbage boards, purses, picture frames, baskets and wine coasters. Quilled lockboxes are also popular on storage boxes with drawers. There are times that this technique is used together with other design methods such as embroidery or printing.

Today, quilling had already started making a comeback. Obviously, it had gone through a lot of changes and transformations as it passes from one generation to another. New styles, materials and techniques are continuously being introduced and this caused a lot of expansion opportunities in the cardmaking industry.

Since more and more people are getting into the art of quilling, more and more types of paper are being produced to give options for quillers. Some paper types are: acid-free quilling paper, graduated quilling papers and two tone quilling papers.

The acid-free quilling paper is a great choice when doing cards or scrapbooks. It is guaranteed to last long without affecting the other elements of your design such as pictures. On the other hand, graduated quilling papers are an exceptional choice for decorations. It has solid colors on the edges, then gradually fades to white. Or it can also have light color as a base then gradually fades to solid or darker color towards the inside. Lastly, the two-tone quilling paper functions very similar to the graduated one, but this one has the same color and varies only in intensity.

Its comeback and increasing popularity in many parts of the world continue to promote the art to people from all cultures, of different ages and walks of life. What used to be an exclusive activity for the elite has become a pleasurable art exercise open for everyone to do.

Paper Type

Quilling paper is available on the consumer market in over 250 colors and measurements. It can be divided into numerous categories, like solid-colored, two-tone, acid-free, and other assorted parcels of quilling paper. It is readily available in various measurements, such as 1/8", 1/4" and 3/8" or 3mm, 5mm, 7mm, and 10mm paper parcels. [8] 5mm being the most widely used size.

Acid-Free

As the name plainly suggests this is a completely acid-free paper. The quality makes it an outstanding choice for making scrapbooks, rubber stamping, and creating frames for images. It guarantees your project to last a lifetime, without any adverse effects on the framed image or album.

Graduated

This kind of paper offers an exceptional want to decorative quilling tasks. The edges have a solid color that gradually fades to white. When using a Graduated paper, a quilling ring begins with a dark shade and faded to a lighter side. On the contrary, some graduated papers begin as white, or a lighter shade, and they later gradually fades into a solid, darker color.

Two-Tone

The appearance consists of a concrete color on one side and a relatively lighter color on the other side. With two-tone paper the color stays the same, however, the strength of the color is different. The main use of this quilling paper is to give a desired level of softness to the quilled subject. It has the capability to quill numerous papers in a single spiral.

The Tools You Will Need

To start with, you should have the materials needed. The essential materials you need in quilling are the quilling paper strips, curling tool and a clear glue. The paper strips are usually lightweight card stock cut into different strips. The standard and most frequently used size is 1/8" but you can have narrower strips like 1/16" or much broader strips such as 1/2" to one inch. The size of the paper strips would depend largely on the design you want. If you desire a style with finer details, the narrower strips would be best. Paper strips are likewise in different colors to improve your designs.

Aside from these 3 materials, you might also need tweezers, a corkboard to work on, pins and toothpicks to help you apply glue to your designs.

Making The Designs

To start, it would be of big help if you have a pattern to base your work on. This will be your guide to quilling your first style. Be patient, as quickly as you have to master the different techniques in making the basic coils, you can have your own time to discover more special designs.

The basic thing to note in paper quilling is to make coils using your curling tool. Depending on the pattern you have, you can make tight coils or lose ones, and you can also make those specialized shapes like the teardrops, the square, the marquis or the eye shape, you can learn them one by one with techniques like pinching the sides of the coiled paper strips to make the shape. The teardrop shape, for instance, which is a typical shape that makes up most quilling designs is made by making a loose coil with your curling tool and pinching one side of it using your thumb and your forefinger to produce a corner on one side, and make it look like a teardrop for a raindrop.

Basically, your style will utilize fundamental shapes like the loose and tight coil. From there, you can make a different ideas of shapes consisting of the spirals and scrolls. You can likewise find ideas on styles and patterns from the internet or from others that will help a lot as your guide to quilling your first art piece.

Mounting Your Design

Dealing with a corkboard can be a fantastic idea to help you pin your design before lastly gluing them on your card or paper. You can make use of a toothpick and tweezers to help put the glue on your finished design and help you install great coils. A clear and fast-drying glue is preferred by many to have a clean finish. As soon as you will be dealing with your own, you will ultimately know the difference and discover your own choice with your materials and tools.

As soon as you mastered this basic guide to quilling, you can then move on to more specialized tasks.

What length of time does Paper Quilling take?

Once you learn the fundamental shapes, it does not take long to make beautiful quilled creations. You can spend hours on larger and more detailed styles if you like. Large quilled patterns are typically masterpieces that stand alone and can be framed for show. Most of the designs you'll most likely make when you are quilling will be smaller products to embellish other crafts you are doing so feel confident that it does not need to take the whole day just to make a few quilled flowers; although your good friends might think so! The terrific aspect of quilling is that it looks a lot more difficult than it really is to do!

Quilling paper is a great way of having fun and a beautiful way to be imaginative with the standard coils and scrolls you'll discover how to make. You'll be happily surprised with the works of art you can produce with just a couple of different kinds of quilled pieces. Simply remember that you need to have a little bit of persistence (especially as a novice quiller) because you are working with little tools and small notepads. Each small coil or scroll will be simply one small part of the total design.

Remember to have fun and make your designs as comprehensive and intricate as you'd like. Take time for some trial and error as you learn and you'll quickly be impressed at how rapidly you can make some really cool quilled styles.

Advanced quillers might spend hours and days or even weeks to produce a really involved style. Some are even 3 dimensional which is actually neat however of course takes a fair bit more time to be elaborate and so comprehensive.

CHAPTER TWO

Materials And Tools Required For Paper Quilling

Quilling is such a versatile art that you can use it anywhere. You can make quilled greeting cards, photo frames, name tags, invitations, scrapbooks. You can also use shapes made by quilling to decorate a box or a flower vase. Or simply you can take a beautiful sheet, make a quilling pattern on it and get it framed to be hanged. The list of its uses is endless. The creativity is yours. You can also make 3D models by quilling as the coiled paper is strong enough and does not get squashed.

Quilling Paper Strips

These come in an untold variety of colours and also in different widths. The most commonly used width is 1/8inch however you can also purchase strips that measure 1/4inch, 1/2inch and 3/4inch. These are used mainly for making fringed flowers or creating 3D pieces.

You can cut the paper strips yourself however, they must be cut with great accuracy otherwise the coils will not look as good. For this reason it is probably more practical to buy paper already cut for you.

Needle Tools and Slotted Quilling Tools

These should be the first tools you get and you may find, depending on the patterns you want to make, that you can stick with just these two for quite a while.

Scissors

You will also find out that you need scissors in a minimalist kit in order to cut your paper strips to the right size or even make your own strips.

Circle Template Board

Since the circle or coil is the basic shape for most patterns, a circle template board can be another useful early addition to any quillers' toolkit as it enables you to accurately measure the sizes of different circles and therefore make more precise designs.

Tweezers

Tweezers are useful for handling your different quilling shapes, especially coils, when working carefully and creating more intricate designs.

A Curling Tool

You can use several different items to curl the strips of paper into coils. Some people use hat pins, toothpicks,a slotted quilling tool or a needle quilling tool. If you use the pins or needle type tools you will have to start the coil by rolling the paper around the center of the tool. When you are a beginner this can actually be quite difficult to perfect so purchasing a slotted quilling tool is probably a good idea. The paper is gripped in the slot making it easier to roll and keep the tension right to produce the correct size of coil. The only slight disadvantage is that the slotted quilling tool had a tendency to leave a little bend at the end of the paper in the middle of the coil.

Glue

Everyone has their preference of which type of glue they prefer to use. The only advice I can give is in the beginning to choose a good quality craft glue that is white and tacky in substance. Be sure that it turns clear when dry. Craft glue is another essential that you need in order to start as it will hold your coils together and is also essential in creating other shapes. If you are starting with a minimalist toolkit then craft glue and a needle tool or slotted tool are your most basic items.

Once you become accustomed to making paper coils you can use any sort of item to curl the paper - many seasoned quillers do finger rolling too!

Quilling Crafts Board

This is not really an essential item but one which will make life a little easier. This board gives you molds of numerous sizes which you can drop your coils into so that they can open up to a uniform size.

Quilling Fringer

Again possibly a non essential however if you wish to create say fringed flowers this tool will allow you to cut the quilling paper quickly and easily.

Fringing tools are ideal for creating beautiful flowers as they make small fringes/cuts in your strips of paper which are often used to make different types of flowers.

Quilling Comb

Once you become more ambitious and you are ready to learn a different quilling crafts technique this tool can help you make zig zag shapes and cascading loops.

CHAPTER THREE

List Of Things That Can Be Made From The Craft Of Paper Quilling

Quilled flowers are really popular because they are so gorgeously made with paper quilling, you will quickly discover that there are so numerous more patterns that you can quill besides simply flowers. Just about anything you can consider, you can quill! From animals to lettering to cars and trucks, you can quill all sorts of patterns using the standard quilling shapes (coils and scrolls) you have found out how to make. The possibilities are actually unlimited considering that you have complete control over the way you develop a style with the fundamental quilling shapes. Quilling is an art type so similar to any other art, you can make anything you'd like and have your ended up piece of artwork appearance unique. Quilling designs can be used to jazz up any scrapbook or card, even for kids, because you can quill all kinds of toys, automobiles, animals, and other products that bit boys enjoy to decorate the pages of their scrapbook. Just like scrapbooks can have a variety of styles, so can your quilled creations. You can make quilled lettering or style concepts for each page of your scrapbook or homemade card no matter what style, season, or holiday you are celebrating. Try to make all types of different patterns and images when you find out the basics of coiling paper and you will quickly discover that your creativity will cut loose method beyond paper flowers. You'll certainly want to try making a variety of animals, trees, cars and trucks, Christmas designs, and so far more.

Pretty soon people will be appreciating your work and using it as inspiration for their quilling projects.

1. **Paper Quilled Monogram**

Experiment and have fun with different shapes and techniques to develop this simple but effective monogram. The innovative freedom is all yours as soon as you have your outline.

2. Autumn Tree Greeting Card

Celebrate the autumn season by sending your buddies welcoming cards embellished with a lovely quilled fall tree. Even if you have never made a quilled craft before, you will have the ability to create this card in no time. It is simply made from eye-shaped quilled coils to represent the leaves and fundamental coiled strips to make the trunk of the tree. The simpleness of the design radiates elegance, and the best part is the tree is so easy to make.

3. Quilled Snowflakes

It's never ever early to begin thinking about Christmas crafting. Collect the kids and make these beautiful quilled snowflakes to decorate your Christmas tree. They are so lovely, you can even use them as affordable gifts for individuals on your Christmas list. Nearly everyone will treasure a gift that you made with your hands, it makes the present that far more special.

4. Quilled Ombre Colored Teardrop Vase

This stylish quilled teardrop vase is a terrific task for starting quillers. Simply glue teardrop shapes in gradients of color onto a vase. This job can be made in under an hour. Who doesn't enjoy a craft job that's quick and easy, however still looks so upscale?

5. Quilled Paper Posies in a Basket

This quilled basket of flowers has a sweet vintage appeal. Frame it for a charming new piece of wall art to await your house or to give away as a gift.

6. Contemporary Quilled Angel

Kids, and adults too, can make this modern quilled angel in less than 15 minutes. Can you think of an entire Christmas tree adorned with these angels from top to bottom? Because they are so easy to make, it's certainly possible. You can rapidly craft enough for your entire "Angel Tree" in a number of hours.

7. Green and Gold Quilled Teardrop Earrings

Make some earrings on your own or for a present. Paper Zen shows how to add a golden metal shimmer to your quilled earrings to give them an extra little bit of enjoyment.

8. Quilled Flowers Decorating a Cake

The next time you need to make a cake for a unique event, decorate it with crepe paper kumquat branches sprinkled with the cutest quilled daisies.

9. Quilled Flower Pendant

Paper quilling naturally offers itself to jewelry tasks. This gorgeous pendant is made up of pink and blue eye shapes around a circular coil. Glue on a pearl and you're done. Little ladies will love this project.

10. Quilled Toy Paper Tops

Quilling can even be used for toy making. Youngsters will be delighted with this paper leading craft. All you need to do is make a round paper coil for the bottom of the top, and after that construct a wall of paper to form the base.

11. Colorful Paper Flower Frame

Are you searching for an affordable but yet impressive gift to give to someone? This quilled paper frame might just be the best answer for you! Glue quilled flowers around a thrifty frame and you'll instantly have a gorgeous gift.

CHAPTER FOUR

Guide To Making Your Own Handmade Card Design, Bracelets And Other Through Quilling

Handcrafted cards typically come from an idea and materialize into an actual product. It usually starts with carving interesting shapes with scissors and then changing the material into an entirely different product altogether.

There are so many different colours, patterns, textures, and forms available for one to create handcrafted cards. Inspiration can come from many other craft hobbies such as origami, quilling, paper mâché, and pop-up storybooks.

Other inspirations for card designs stem from everyday surroundings outside in nature, through clothing styles and trends in fashion, and life experiences. Occasions can also be inspirational. Common events such as birthdays, weddings, showers, mother's day, father's day, and Christmas.

Once you get inspired to create a card, creativity is another difficult challenge to overcome. What materials to use and how to make it are the first things that come to mind. Determine what you have available and what you need. You already probably have the occasion in mind, so think about who you are actually making the card for. Reflect back on their personality and interest and add something to it you think they'll like. If it's a birthday, maybe make the theme one of their favourite hobbies. If it's a Christmas card, make the theme a winter sport they like. There are endless possibilities, that is why handcrafted cards can be so personal and custom.

As you become better at creating cards, you may branch out into the business of creating them for others and selling them. This industry continues to grow as personalization is a unique offering for those special occasions. However, practice your inspiration, ideas and creativity before venturing into this field. Understanding how what to use, how to use and what looks best is important in commercializing a handcrafted card business.

The following steps are methods to make the main shapes.

1. Firstly, place a wax paper sheet on your work surface. Then, remove a piece of quilling paper to the proper size like the project pattern.

2. Put the last part of quilling paper on the tool like a corsage pin.

3. To produce a circle shape, hold the paper with your thumb and forefinger. Next, twist it and turn the tool. It will wind up into a tight circle. Continue turning and construct a larger circle. Hold it and glue the ripped end to link it.

4. If you wish to produce a loose circle, cut the length of the material. Roll it to the tool and remove it.

5. To make a teardrop shape, you must turn the loose circle. Glue the end and hold the end with your thumb and forefinger. Then, squeeze the end to construct a teardrop shape.

6. For making a marquise shape, very first glue the end of the circle and hold it. Twist both ends to develop a marquise shape.

7. Meanwhile to make a square, roll a loose circle and glue the end. Pinch the both sides by turning the piece and turn two opposite locations to build the square.

8. You can start to make a teardrop shape and glue ending to form a triangle. Squeeze two points with thumb and forefinger to construct triangle.

9. To develop a flower and patterns, simply glue shaped pieces together. You are permitted to select quilled pieces with tweezers.

Quilling Instructions For Quilling Craft Beginners

In the beginning, it is an excellent idea to use a slotted quilling tool as this will make things a bit much easier. As you grow in confidence and development you may want to change to using a needle or a toothpick.

One needs to carefully place the end of a quilling paper strip into the slot of the quilling tool. Ensure that you hold the quilling tool with the hand you use professionally and the paper should be held between your forefinger and thumb. Thoroughly and gradually in the beginning turn the quilling tool, winding the paper round the idea uniformly and with the edges level.

When you have actually rolled enough paper to make the size of coil you desire hold it for a minute or so, let go of the paper and tip the tool over to permit the paper coil to drop onto your work area. Do not get tense when the paper begins to unravel a little, this will always occur.

Before gluing the end of the paper coil, it is best to allow it to unwind and uncoil itself a little. When you are sure it has stopped use a cocktail stick or something comparable to put an extreme percentage of tacky glue onto the end of the paper and stick it into place.

Do not get stressed if your very first couple of coils are not best, it takes practice!

Once you have your coil shapes it is then time to pinch and squeeze them into the shapes you need to develop a picture.

Pro Quilling Tips Every Beginner Should Know

When you are learning to quill, it is natural for you to want your completed quilling to look precisely like the pattern you are following, however it most likely will not. There are lots of elements that affect the look of a quilled piece that a lot of artists are not even understanding. Here are five quilling pointers that discuss the issues you might be having and what you can do to create more constant, professional quillwork that you can be happy with.

Your scrolls and rolls will be special to you. They will not look exactly like mine or like those of anyone else. When they curl the paper strips resulting in variations in the scrolls and coils, everyone utilizes various tension. Not just that, but your own quills will differ from each other depending upon your state of mind and how you feel at the time. To see for yourself, compare coils that you made when you are tired out or exhausted with those made when you are unwinded and rested. You'll see a big distinction. A great tip is to prepare all of your strips for a task at one time. This permits you to roll your strips one right after the other, producing quills with more constant tension.

Neatness counts, control the glue. Absolutely nothing will ruin the appearance of a piece of finished quilling more than seeing little bits of glue all over it or gobs of glue under it where it is connected to its backing. It just takes the smallest drop to seal the end of a coil to itself or to attach one coil or scroll to another as you build your design. A bit more adhesive might be needed to attach the paper quilling to the box or frame back, but very little. When working with paper filigree and you'll desire to clean your hands before beginning on any quilling job, tidy hands are an absolute must. The very best quilling suggestion I've found to assist keep glue off the fingers is to keep a wet paper towel convenient to wipe your fingers on as you quill. Also, keep cold cream to a minimum so the oils don't tarnish the paper.

All quilling paper is not produced equal. You would think that one package of 1/8 inch wide paper would be the same as another, however that's not the case. As all of us understand, paper is available in different weights and even among those of the very same weight, some documents simply have more "body" than others making them more suitable for quilling. The weight of the paper used to produce the strips will differ somewhat between producers and even within the exact same maker. In fact, there is one producer out there offering quilling strips made from thin card stock that is very difficult to work with because it cracks and divides. If you are having a problem with quilling, before you quit out of aggravation, try a strip of paper from various businesses. You might find that the issue with your coils is with the paper and not you.

Quilling paper has a "right" and a "wrong" side. If you analyze a strip of quilling paper, you will observe that one side has smooth edges that curve down ever so somewhat. The opposite has edges that a little curve up. This is since the paper cutting blade lowers on the paper as it cuts. The smooth side is thought about the right (or top) side of the paper. You will want to start your curls with this side of the paper up. This distinction is especially visible when joining a number of strips together to form a large tight coil for usage as a base, and so on.

Use the quilling tool that works for you. There are numerous industrial tools readily available for curling paper, both straight and slotted needle types. A round toothpick or corsage pin can be used also.

Quilling tools are just that; tools to help you create the preferred coil or spiral. By all means, follow the directions that come with the tool or those you discover online, however if the instructions simply do not seem to work for you, do not hesitate to try using the tool in a slightly different method.

If you are still using a specific kind of tool, try a different tool completely. You will quickly find the one that is right for you.

Put these quilling suggestions to work for you and you'll see enhanced results in no time.

CHAPTER FIVE

Birthday Card Or Invitation Card

You can make beautiful invitations in minutes with the kids, not only is it a fun and easy craft for kids, but it will save money as well. Plus. With just a few materials, you can make cards like these in minutes.

Materials needed to make party invitations

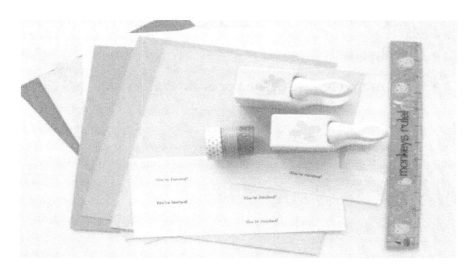

Gather the supplies you will need to make these cute party invitations. You will only need a few simple products to make these cute party invitations:

- Colored paper (you can use weight paper for text or, for a more paper-like appearance, use cardstock paper)
- Flower punch (any flower shape of your choice; these flowers were made with the hydrangea flower)
- Small dots of glue
- Ruler (you can use the ruler to give the cards a nice and neat fold)
- Scissors or paper cutters (to cut an 8 1/2 "x 11" sheet of paper in half and fold each half into a card)
- Washi tape
- Alternatively, use tissue paper flowers.

Steps:

1. Use a paper punch to create flower shapes

Make paper flower petals with your flower punch.

Next, take your paper flower piercings and make some paper flowers. (Note: you can use petals of the same size to stack on top of each other to create 3-dimensional flowers; however, using different-sized petals provides a more realistic look.)

2. Start making your own flowers

Use glue dots or a bead of glue to create your flower base.

Use a small dot of glue or a bead of glue to start assembling the base of your flower. Stack the main petals slightly flipped over the lower one so that the lower petals are visible.

3. Include more petals to finish your flower

Glue the rest of the petals together to form the flower. Add more petals of smaller size, using multi-colored paper for the smallest petal for the top center.

4. Here are some finished paper flowers

Your flowers will look like this.

Create lots of beautiful paper flowers in various colors. Place them on the celebration invitations and save the extra flowers in a box for later use. You can put these pretty paper flowers on thank you cards, birthday cards, celebration table placement cards, gift bags, or anything else you want to consider. The possibilities are limitless!

5. Include washi tape on your paper

Add some washi tape to your card and print or write the message on the front of the card.

Be sure to include the following information within your invitation to the celebration:

- Where (full address)
- Date (date and day of the week)
- Time (what time it ends and begins)
- RSVP information (your email and/or phone number).

Similarly, you may want to include any other information that visitors might need, such as how the children should dress, or the style of the party.

6. Timeless and fun outdoor party games

Produce multiple party invitations in a variety of colors. Interact with others to choose various colors of paper and washi tape patterns to produce a batch of party invitations. Let your creativity shine as you create beautiful cards in whatever you choose.

CHAPTER SIX

Making Of Bracelets And Necklaces

Most people are probably familiar with feathered flowers and leaves, however the method can also be used to develop beautiful, lightweight, and durable precious jewelry.

Yes, paper is a perfectly ideal product for earrings and bracelets, It is extraordinarily strong when rolled up and the finished parts can be further enhanced with fixative.

Styles made with rolled paper strips are getting more sophisticated which motivates people to try this awesome type of paper art.

To get an idea of how to roll jewelry paper, cut strips from a sheet of paper and roll them one at a time between your thumb and forefinger. With practice, the pressure. Some quillers don't use tools for measurement, they just depend on their fingers. However, most people crave to work with a needle tool or slit tool.

The needle tool takes longer to master, however the result will be a perfectly round bobbin. A superfine fluted tool is my favorite as it produces a little curl.

The materials used to make precious quilling jewelry include; paper strips and glue, they are simple and inexpensive to get.

Any type of glue suitable for paper will be ideal for quilling and you will be surprised how little is needed. My favorite gluing method is to put some clear adhesive gel on the lid of a plastic container. Since it does not affect skin when exposed to air, I prefer gel to white glue.

To prevent glue from blocking the tip as you work, place it upside down in a votive candle holder or cup lined with a damp paper cloth. A damp cloth is also useful for cleaning sticky fingers.

When the specific shapes of the pens are finished, arrange them with tweezers on a tray or corkboard and glue them one at a time. You can use pins to hold the shapes in place until the glue is dry. Flip the piece over to use featured glue dots on the seams and apply a light fixative when you finish if you prefer.

A clean Styrofoam tray is great for organizing and gluing feathered pieces. Last but not least, attach the results to the pieces.

Step 1: Material Required

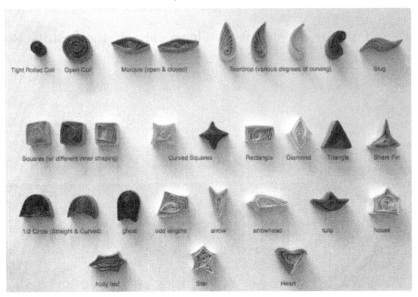

Step 3: To Begin With..

Step 4: Assemble Your Earrings

Step 5: Make. Wear. Flaunt.

63

CHAPTER SEVEN

Wall Décor

Craft enthusiasts often think about how to make a stunning wall design using the quilling technique. The Art of Quilling includes many simple floral designs. When it comes to discovering a beginner-friendly Quilling style, leaves and flowers are the best choices you can make, in the middle of it all.

Quilling styles for wall frames should be attractive and have a beautiful look. Quilling art and colorful, elegant Quilling design are wonderful when handcrafted.

Quilling, weaving, and shelling. All of these technical components combine to produce a fantastic coat rack that anyone with knowledge of the basic ways of quilling and shelling could make. The weaving is in basic patterns and the use of this intriguing technique adds dimension and depth.

The flowers are simple and eccentric marquises shapes, with yellow skins to accentuate. The leaves are shaped like a dark green and dark green marquise. Yellow accents are rolls of glue of various lengths, glued together.

Another type of wall hanging is the wreath. This popular hanging design works well for parties, as seasonal tags, and appears in almost any room in many homes. The bow is a simple collection of narrow strips, some loosely rolled to create a ribbon effect. The use of various types of flower making techniques brings additional interest to this design.

Wall hangings can be suspended within metal or wooden rings, using thread or tape to hold the piece in place. The feathers can be attached to the cord that is grasped and held tightly in a needle loop.

Any preparation for a wreath can have padded shapes glued to it, producing pieces that can reflect and spice up the holiday or your home area. And the designs are limited only by your imagination and the decision to create something that is yours alone.

We will go a step further with our flowers, developing independent designs that do not need paper support, the frame or the wall as support. An important tool in these projects is florist wire, which can be gotten from artisan stores. If you cannot find such a thread, you can use a fairly light craft thread; just cover it with a green flower wrap or bandana to hide the metal. The eccentric white marquise and the tears are used to imitate a basket, so that the cork seems to be the "foot" of it. The flowers are twisted pinks, small tufted flowers, and extremely small bunny ears with tight spiral centers. The leaves are cut and engraved. All shapes are mounted on wires and pressed in artisan polystyrene.

Let's take a look at how to make floral wall decorations use Quilling Art.

Materials needed:

- Thermocol Sheet
- Stairs
- Quilling strips
- Quilling needle
- Adhesive

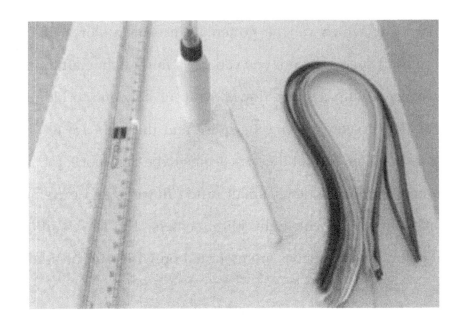

Steps:

1. Create the base

Take a sheet of thermocol and cut it to the size of 30 * centimeters on each side, giving you a square of thermocol.

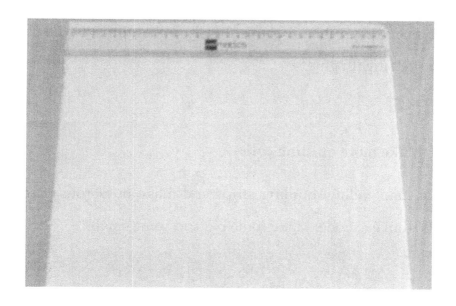

2. Let's make a double shadow filigree coil

Start by joining an orange stripe with 3-4 stripes to create a long double shadow Quilling stripe. This will give you a double shadow coil as shown in the picture.

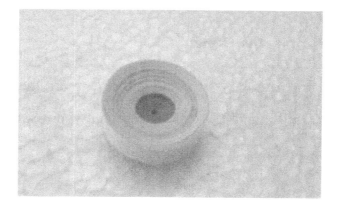

Take the quilling needle and make tight coils with it and secure the end of the coil with glue. Lightly push the starter coils to get a styling coil as shown above. Put it in the center of the sheet and stick it with glue.

3. Make more quilling coils

Take some yellow quilling strips and make numerous narrow coils from each one. Make some big and some small.

4. Start creating the Design

Now take the orange strip and stick it with the adhesive, keeping the quilling strip vertical. Attach a yellow spiral to the end of the petal.

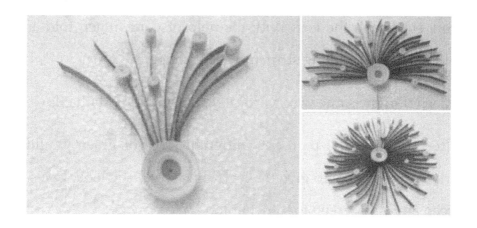

Place a second, smaller petal next to the first, using the same method. Make the floral pattern in such a way that all of your petals appear consistent even after being of different sizes. Strategically glue the narrow yellow spirals in the middle, to provide the designer with the Quilling pattern.

5. Create leaves for the flower

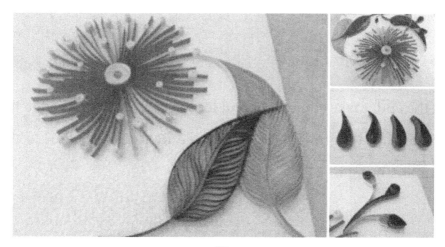

Now start with the leaf. With the help of your finger, fold and fold the green Quilling strip into a leaf shape.

Attach it in the same way, vertically, as you did with the flower.

After applying the pan, cut different sizes of green Quilling strips accordingly, to give the leaf veins a realistic look. Use sap green and dark green for a richer look.

6. Give it a final touch

In the end, make some tight and loose orange coils and edge the sheet with a thermal neck to provide more information to the Quilling design.

7. Your creation is ready!

And that is it! A stunning wall decor with handcrafted Quilling art and handmade by you. It just takes a little patience to make this lovely Quilling-style wall frame, but the effort is definitely worth the wait.

Make this Quilling art style a part of your home design and watch the world in awe of your talent!.

CHAPTER EIGHT

Types Of Quilling Patterns And Project Ideas

If you are completely new to quilling, try these simple quilling ideas.

1. Quilling narrow circles

One of the easiest quilling designs to create is a simple, tight circle, secured in place with a glue. This shape is produced by inserting quilling strips into the slotted end of a quilling tool, then wrapping the strips around the tool before removing it.

2. Quilling loose circles

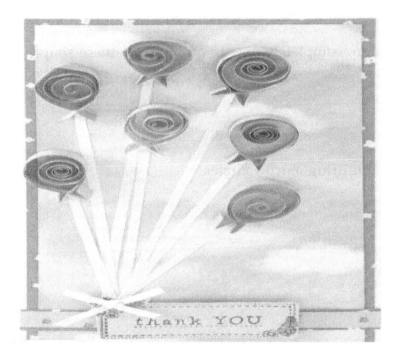

To produce these fun feathered balloons, simply start to develop a tight circle with feathers, as in the previous work, but instead of gluing the ends together, let the tension in the circle loosen slightly, to reveal a swirling circular design. , before gluing the free end. instead. Squeeze one end of the balloon a little to give it more shape, then whistle a small strip of paper and glue it to the pinched end. Also include thin strips of paper to represent the strings of the balloons.

3. Quilling teardrops

This flexible shape can be used for many different styles. You can use it to develop leaves on this cute wreath card. To develop the shape, simply pinch the glued end of a loose circle to form a point.

4. Quilling squares and hearts

To create the square cake tiers on this wedding card, pinch two opposite sides of a circle with loose feathers into points, rotate the pinched circle 90 degrees, and then pinch two more points on the remaining rounded sides. To make the sweet feathered hearts, fold a quilling strip in half, unfold it to form a "V," then curl the ends inward.

5. Diamond quilling

To get the diamond shape, simply make a quilted square, then apply light pressure to two opposite corners. You can mix teardrop and diamond shapes to create a quilted floral embellishment for a label.

6. Quilling rolls

Similar to heart designs, you can form the ends of a folded quilling strip so that they curve outward. The flower heads were formed by surrounding a small loose circle with rings of quilling strips.

7. Quilling lockets and earrings

Just like quilling on cards, you can also make some amazing quilling jewelry, like this quilling pendant. Start by cutting a shape out of paper, then drape a strip of quilling paper several times around the outside. Make a range of small loose circles in different colors, to fit the shape, then include the 3D glitter on top to seal it in.

8. How to quill your A, B, C

From abstract patterns to intricate wildlife designs and fairy tales, let your creativity run free. Draw the selected letter and carefully glue the edge of the quilling strips around it. Surround the letter with your choice of quilt shapes to develop this colorful decoration.

9. Let your creativity fly with feathered birds

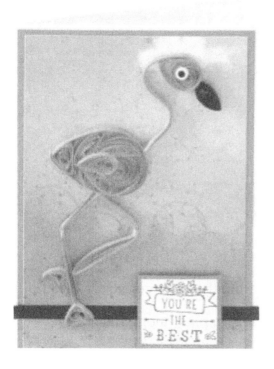

Use quilted shapes to develop characters on your cards, such as birds or other wild animals. This stunning flamingo is made up of a series of loose circles and tears in different sizes, as well as strips of quilling paper folded lengthwise for the neck and legs. You can pair the quilted flamingo with our fabulous tropical bird pattern cards.

10. Quilling greeting Cards

Start writing greetings with the scrolling technique. Write your choice in pencil initially, then cut strips of quilling paper, curl the ends, and glue it in place along the edges.

11. Quilling snowflakes

12. Quilling vase

Spice up an old vase with these ombre paper drops.

13. Quilling of hearts

Write your design and then glue it to paper for a gift or frame it for your wall.

14. Quilling for Christmas

15. Quilling frames

16. Acorn quilling

CHAPTER NINE

Photo Frame

A great and simple way to spend lots of time with your children and help them contribute to a home improvement task. The photo frame looks lovely as a mantelpiece and even as a gift.

Required materials:

- Cardboard, paper or cardboard, color of your choice

- Scale / ruler

- Paper cutter

- Eraser

- Pencil

- Glue

- Handmade paper / expensive paper

- Quilled Flowers

- And a lot of illusion!

Steps:

1. Cut the front and back pieces of paper

Mark 7 inches wide and 6 inches tall on the paper card, using a pencil and a scale / rule.

Cut the paper with the help of a letter opener, it is best to ask your children to mark the size and you cut it. You will need 2 of these pieces of paper, for the back and front of the photo frame.

Since we are making enough frame for the size of a 4 x 3 inch image, we will need to cut a window out of one of the sheets of paper. Now, to be exceptionally accurate, you'll need to make sure your window is in the center of the sheet of paper.

Create an area using the 4 sided scale / ruler to create the points of a 4 inch x 3 inch rectangular shape for your window. Use the cutter and scale / ruler to help you better cut the required rectangle.

2. Cover the pieces of paper with patterned paper

Once the front window and back cover card stock are ready, we need to cover it with fancy paper or craft paper of your choice. To cover the back of the picture frame, use glue gently to stick the expensive paper onto the sheet of paper. Now to make sure the card is fully covered, make sure your fancy card is larger than your sheet of paper. Use the gift wrap approach as an envelope to cover the piece.

For the front of the sheet of paper, use expensive, light-colored paper. Put the front of the frame on the patterned paper and just one inch larger than our frame. Please mark a square smaller than our window in the picture frame and cut out the paper. Make grooves at all four corners and inside the patterned paper so that it is folded and adhered to the frame. Apply the glue generously and you now have both the front and back of the picture frame in place.

3. Bring the front and back of the photo frame together

Glue the 2 pieces of the front and back frame now ready. Please note that you need to glue only 3 sides and leave one side open, so you can move on to the photo of your choice.

4. Decorate the photo frame

Quilted flowers and leaves produce colorful decorations.

These can be used to decorate anything, straight from paper bags, gift bags, boxes, and of course, photo frames.

Use a variety of padded flowers and leaves to produce a few bunches to spruce up your frame. Now what I've actually done is use the corners of my image frame to accentuate the look, but you can completely hide the sides of the frame to your liking.

To make the backing, use cardstock or cardstock, glue it to a larger sheet, and fold. It depends on whether you want your frame to be vertical or horizontal. Conveniently, you will need to glue the bracket to the frame.

Hope you enjoy quilling and item crafting with your family and friends.

CHAPTER TEN

Teardrop Vase

This stylish quilled teardrop vase is an amazing project for starting quillers. Just glue teardrop shapes in gradients of color onto a vase. This job can be made in under an hour. Who does not love a craft job that's simple and fast, but still looks so upscale. Changing paper rolls into quilling shapes is as simple as pinching one or more sides. How many sides are pinched, and how close these sides are, is what identifies the end result. Tearsdrop are a great place to start handling quilling shapes, because they are simply a matter of gently squeezing one side of the loose coil. Some shapes even have slight variations.

Steps:

1. Fold the tip of your teardrop between your fingers and you have created a shaped teardrop

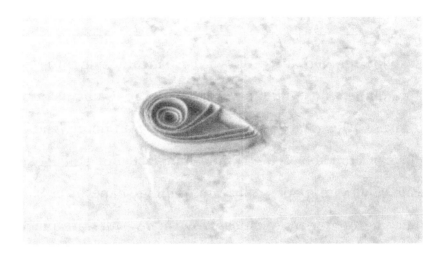

2. Tears are the best sheets or starting point for these quilling paper snowflakes

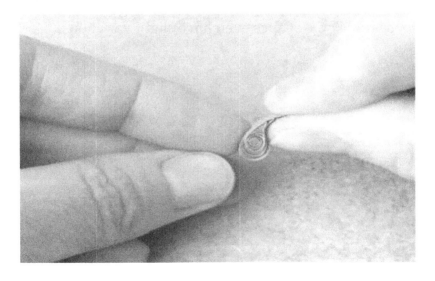

3. Pinch two opposite ends of a loose spiral at the same time to develop a marquise

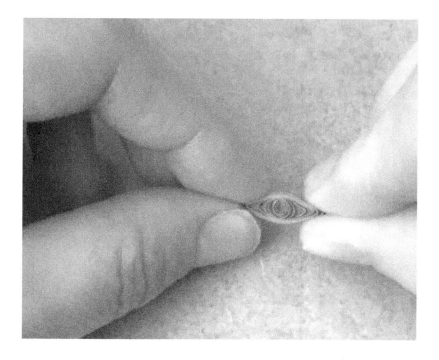

As in the case of the shaped teardrop, flexing the marquise will form a new shape!

4. **This time, use both hands to press and flex the marquise tips into an "S" shape.** It is shaped like a marquise.

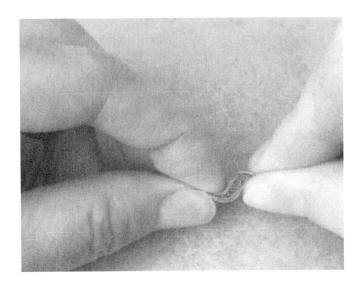

5. Again, starting with a loose coil, pinch both sides, but keep the bottom flat with your thumbs at the same time

The semicircles were the shapes I used to form my white paper lilacs!

This may take a couple of sessions, however you can!

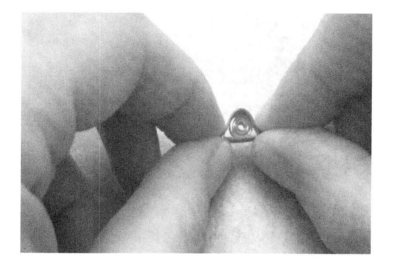

6. From a semicircle you can create a half moon

It is as simple as folding the center of the moon over your thumb.

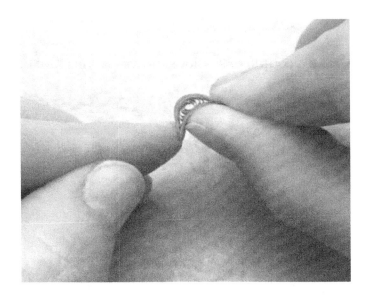

After reviewing some of these new shapes, start tweaking them a bit.

7. Instead of flexing your fingertips, you could possibly use a wooden dowel. When you pinch the center of the coils a bit, notice how they look. I bet you will quickly develop really special and natural shapes!

CHAPTER ELEVEN

Bats

Why not surprise your kids with these intriguing Halloween crafts and have a lovely time together making paper quilled crafts? This Paper Quilled bat craft is extremely enjoyable.

What you need:

- Quilling paper: you can quickly buy it online. You need 3 strips of black paper.
- A quilling tool
- A toothpick: this is the very best way to apply the glue
- Tacky glue
- A ruler: to determine the strip lengths that you need. After some experience, you'll be able to eyeball this
- 2 earring wires
- 2 dive rings - I didn't have any on hand so I made my own with some wire
- Little needle/nosed pliers: for connecting the earring wires and leap rings

- Quilling form *(optional)*: It is not absolutely necessary as you can merely form the coils and size them without it but you might discover it convenient when you begin doing bigger, more elaborate projects.

Steps:

1. **Take a 20 inch long (or longer) quilling strip and use the slotted quilling tool to coil the entire strip.** Get the coil from the tool and allow the coil to loosen up freely. As soon as you are pleased with the coil size, glue the open end of the coil to protect it. Now glue the loose coil on a piece of dark color craft paper; I use grey.

2. Carefully cut the craft paper all around the coils' outer edge

3. Take a 10-inch long quilling strip and produce a loose coil pattern with it

4. Press any one side of the loose coil to form a teardrop shape

5. Now press 2 more sides (on the opposite side of the formerly pushed location) of the teardrop; this will form a triangular shape

6. **Now press and fold in the middle part of any two pressed sides of the triangular shape.** Similarly, create another one of these patterns. These 2 will be the wings of the bat; you will need to create 2 more shapes for the wing.

7. **Take 5 inches long quilling strip and form a triangular shape. Likewise, develop another one.** These 2 will be the ears of the bat.

8. **Use a 5-inch quilling strip to produce 2 lens shapes, 4-inch quilling strips to develop 2 lens shapes and 2-inch quilling strips to create 2 loose coils.** The 2 sets of lens shapes are for the wings and the 2 loose coils will be the legs.

9. Place the ready items on a flat surface to examine the bat pattern

10. Combine the prepared parts one by one by using craft glue

11. **Cut out the eyes, mouth and, fangs of the bat.** Merely use white craft paper to eliminate the eyes and the fangs. Use a black sharpie to draw the eyeballs and use a pink craft paper for the mouth.

12. **Stick the prepared parts on the big loose coil pattern. Enable the glue to dry entirely.** And, done!

CHAPTER TWELVE

Paper Quilled Monogram

With time, practice and a little persistence, you will soon end up being a professional.

Materials:

- Pair of scissors
- Handcrafted paper knife
- Tweezers
- Adhesive glue
- 1 old paper plate or plastic glue container
- Brush
- Pre-cut cardboard or quilling strips in the desired colors
- 1 sheet of thick cardboard or cardboard for the background
- 1 Shadowbox photo frame.

Steps:

1. **Print your Strip.** Print your chosen letter, filled with a light or dark colored background of your choice, on the background of the cardstock

Alternative methods to create letters

If you don't have access to a printer, use this alternative technique for a letter:

i. Trace a large character from a character, such as a book or a magazine, onto a sheet of paper using a pencil.

ii. Use a light touch with the pencil, you don't want to see the pencil lines on your project. It will be difficult to remove the lines after building the frame.

iii. Or you can filled the letter with a favorite background color peeking out from under the covered pieces.

iv. Use a ruler to make the lines straight.

v. Attach the tracing paper to a card for stability, if desired.

2. Cut the strips:

i. Choose the card in the colors you want to integrate into your style.

ii. Use the cutter to cut 1/4 inch wide strips of paper from card stock.

...or buy pre-cut cardboard strips:

Instead of cutting strips, purchase pre-cut quilling paper packets online or at the craft store.

3. **Give the stripes a shape.** When choosing what your letter's interior design will be, it's time to create shapes.

i. Take a strip of paper and wrap it around the toothpick or quilling tool in any way you like, rolled tightly (for a compact shape) or loose, whichever way you prefer.

ii. Put some glue on the end of the paper strip to hold the shape in place.

iii. Before curling the stripes, take a look at other feathered monograms for inspiration and make a quick miniature initial sketch for your monogram design.

Six Common Types of Rolled Quilling Shapes

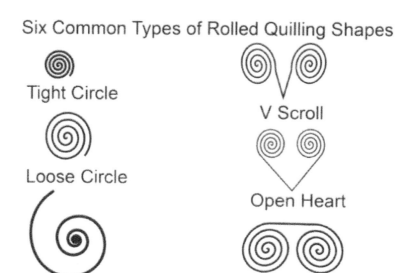

Tight Circle

Loose Circle

Loose Scroll

V Scroll

Open Heart

C Scroll

4. **Outline your letter with strips of paper.** Use your preferred method of applying glue to the pieces of paper that will form the frame of your letter.

Glue: less is better.

Too much glue can destroy your work, so be careful. There are two ways to apply glue to the straight strips of paper that make up the letter frame. Use one of these techniques to place your feathered and shaped pieces inside the letter frame as well:

i. Use a light touch and a small brush to apply the glue to the edge of the paper.

ii. Gently place the strips on a glued paper plate to lightly cover the edge of a piece, then arrange the pan.

5. Frame the outside of the letter with strips of paper:

i. Glue and place your strips in the outline of your letter. Gently hold each strip until the glue is solid enough to allow the paper strip to rise on its own.

ii. Make a neat fold in a strip of paper and attach a drop of glue to each end and overlap each corner. This little strip will set the corners.

iii. Glue and overlap a quarter-inch strip as an anchor anywhere else you join with a strip of paper that creates the wall. The layers will make the frame more powerful.

iv. Let the pen wall dry completely for writing.

6. **Start filling in the frame of your letter.** As soon as you've built the outdoor frame, fill the inside with your monogram.

i. Follow your style and glue the shapes and strips into place, using your fingers and tweezers for tight spaces.

ii. Allow the finished piece to dry completely for a few hours.

7. **Use your tweezers.** Tweezers are a quiller's best friend. They are one of the most important tools you will use because they help you place paper shapes of all sizes in small spaces within your monogram work without interrupting the frame.

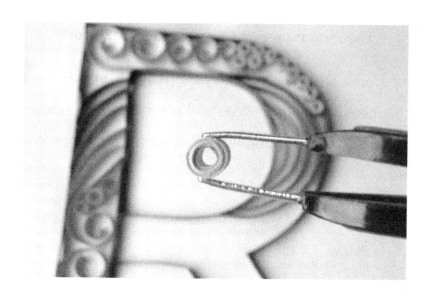

8. **Frame the monogram with the finished quill.** When your piece is dry, place it in the frame of your shadow box.

The importance of a Shadowbox framework

A base frame with glass is not deep enough to accommodate your feathered monogram. You will need a shadow box at least an inch deep to accommodate the raised surface of the pen activity.

CHAPTER THIRTEEN

Paper Quilled Teardrop Vase

What you will need:

- A vase: Preferably a ceramic vase in a simple way, which worked very well. We need an opaque vase, not too big, that does not have severe curves, but soft and gentle curves

- Paper Strips in a Gradient Color - Search online or visit a paper craft store and you will find paper strip sets at an affordable price in a wide range of colors. You will only need one set for a small vase like mine

- Glue: must have the ability to glue the paper to the ceramic

- Grooved Quilling Tool: This is a rod with a groove at the end essentially and it's cheap to buy

- Quilling Needle Tool: You can instead use a cocktail stick or anything with a tip that can apply glue correctly

- Quilling board *(optional)* - Very convenient to have to make sure the tears are the same size. However, you could use a ruler or just draw a circle on paper to use as a guide

- Convenient to have: tweezers to move difficult objects and a cotton swab to clean glue on the go.

Steps:

1. **Roll up the paper spirals**

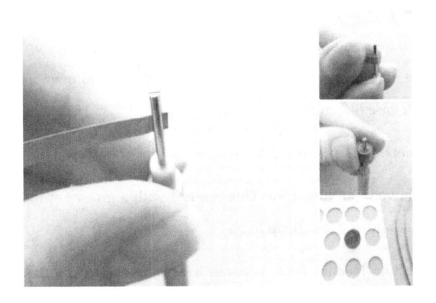

- Starting with the darkest paper color to use, place the end of a paper strip in the slitting tool.

- You want to rotate the tool by holding the paper strip so that the paper wraps tightly around the metal rod.

- It's not critical, however, the paper strips have a smoother side and a rougher side, so try to keep the smoother side on the outside of the spiral.

- While rotating the tool, hold the forming reel with your finger to check it and prevent it from becoming loose or dirty.

- Place the bobbin in a circle on the quilling board and let it slowly unfold to fill the hole-shaped guide after turning the entire strip into a bobbin. I used the third hole down, which is 17mm in diameter.

- If you don't have a quilling board, you can use a drawn circular guide or ruler and let the coil loosen until it reaches the desired size.

- Then you need to put some glue on the end of the paper strip, inside, to hold the spool due to its shape. You can use a quilling needle or cocktail to apply the glue accurately.

2. Form the tears

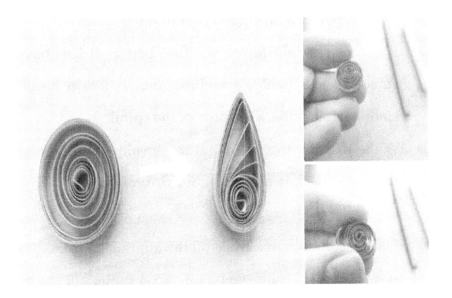

- You have to take each of the coils you make and then turn them into a teardrop shape.

- This is really easy and all you have to do is gently squeeze the center of the coil between your index finger and thumb and pinch one end to create a sharp crease.

- It depends on you what size you make your tears and it mainly depends on the size of your vase. I made 4 rows of one size and then made smaller size tears for the top row.

3. Add the tears to the jar

- Make a handful of feathered tears to start. Then start gluing them to your vase, starting from the base.

- Just use some glue on the back (mainly the top and bottom) and hold the tear on the surface of the jar for a moment. It should stick pretty fast.

- When you have finished a row, you can duplicate all the steps with a different color and create the next row. And after that, duplicate all of this on your vase or until you don't want the design to be completed.

4. Finished!

In fact, you have now finished your beautiful feathered vase!

CHAPTER FOURTEEN

Paper Quilled Flower Cake

Quilling simply involves winding paper ribbons into decorative shapes to produce an intricate 3-D resulting pattern. And as you might have thought, any pattern that can be produced with strips of paper can just as much be created with strips of gum paste or modeling paste and used in cake design.

You can even include more rolled strips to make these flowers look "fuller."

To make these feathered flowers, you will need the following supplies:

OPTION ONE

- Red gum paste or 50/50.

- Light blue or 50/50 gum paste.

- Yellow or 50/50 gum paste.

- Paint brush.

- Water.

- Embossing mat.

- Circle cutter.

- Pizza cutter or strip cutter.

- Roller.

Steps:

1. **Start rolling red and light blue or 50/50 gum paste**

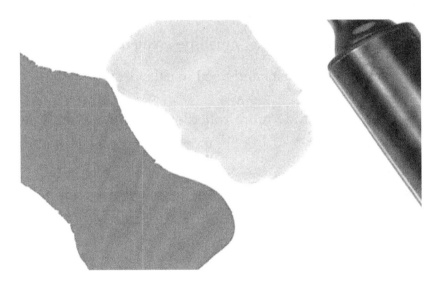

2. **Use a pizza cutter or fondant strip cutter to remove numerous strips.** My strips were half an inch wide and about 3 inches long

3. **Brush some water onto one end of the strip only**

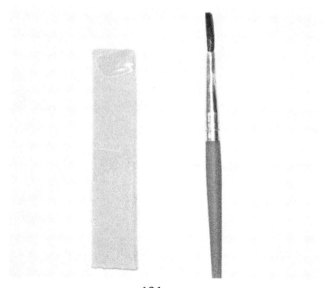

4. Fold the strip in a loop upward until both ends stick together

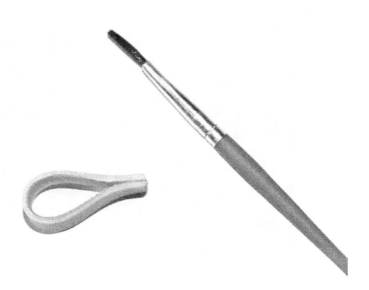

5. Repeat steps 3 and 4 for all remaining strips

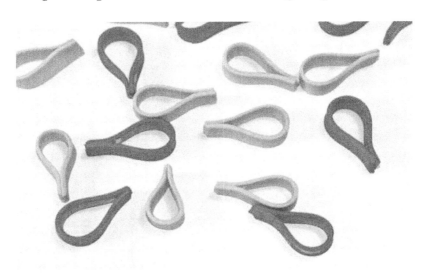

6. **Now, spread on some yellow or 50/50 gumpaste.** Lay an embossing mat on top and press up firmly until the pattern transfers to the gum paste.

7. **Use a circular cutter to remove some pieces.** Each flower will need 2 of these circular pieces.

8. **Flip one of the circular pieces over so that the raised side is facing down.** Brush some water all over this piece.

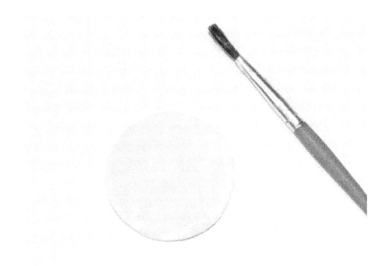

9. Set all the blue and red ties around the circle

10. Brush some water onto another circular piece and glue it on top of the loops

You can also glue a lollipop stick through these flowers with some gumpaste glue or melted chocolate if you like. Then allow these pieces to dry overnight or until set and use on your cakes and cupcakes.

OPTION TWO

Materials:

- White printer paper
- Yellow paper
- Glue stick
- Scissors and / or paper cutter.

Steps:

1. For a fringed center, cut a piece of yellow cardstock (1.5cm X 3cm) and border the edge. Roll it up and protect it with a little glue

2. For flower petals, cut 1/4 " strips of printer paper

3. Roll the strip into a tight coil, let it unwind a bit, and secure it with a little glue

4. With 2 fingers, pinch the circular coil at the ends so that the shape ends up being more of a diamond

5. Keep making the diamond shapes until you have enough petals

6. To make a double diamond petal, make two diamond coils and flatten them, protecting them by wrapping

another strip of paper around the outer edge of the two pieces and gluing them in place

7. Glue all the finished petals around the rolled or fringed centerpiece.

CHAPTER FIFTEEN

Paper Quilling Flower Pendant

If you just love creating different and unconventional fashion jewelry, try this paper flower pendant. It's amazing and easy to do, you don't need to know how to make fancy jewelry to try it on!

Paper quilling is a fun hobby, and supplies are so cheap! You can use purchased quilling strips or make your own, you want to keep a texture and therefore it can be boring.

Once you're done making this paper flower pendant, try it out with other styles. Make it into a keyring, make smaller versions like earrings, and combine a few quilt patterns to make an eye-catching necklace or bracelet.

What you need to make a paper quilling flower pendant:

- Quilling paper strips
- Glue
- Crevice tool for quilling
- 4mm synthetic pearl *(optional)*

- Jump ring

- Chain or full cord

- *Optional*: additional beads to decorate the chain.

Steps:

1. **Select a strip of paper in your first color and use the watermark tool to wrap the strip**

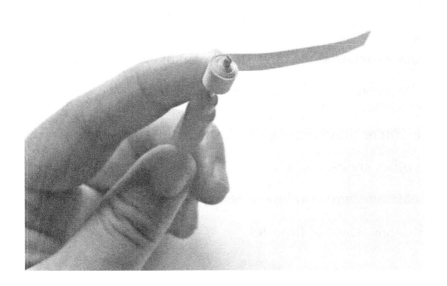

2. After tightly wrapping the entire strip, remove it from the quilling tool, holding the strip so that it does not unroll

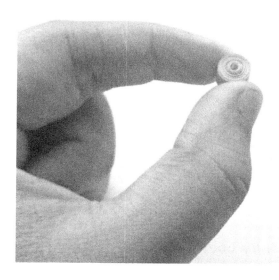

3. Let the coil loosen up

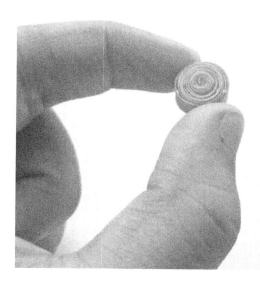

4. **Lay the spiral strip on a flat surface and glue a small bead to the center of the quilted circle** *(optional)*

5. **Retighten the coil by holding it between 2 fingers and pulling the open end.** As soon as the core has tightened, wrap the rest of the strip around and apply glue to the tip to protect the coil. This will be the center of the paper quilling flower

6. Select a quilling strip in the second color and apply it using the slit quilling tool

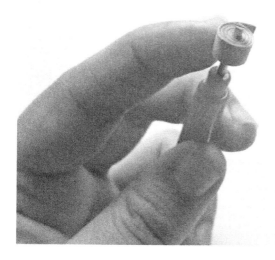

7. After quilling the strip, carefully remove it from the tool

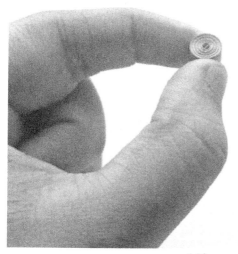

8. **Allow the coil to loosen slightly by placing it on a flat surface**

9. **Take the pattern loose and pinch one side to get a pointed edge.** You are now teardrop-shaped

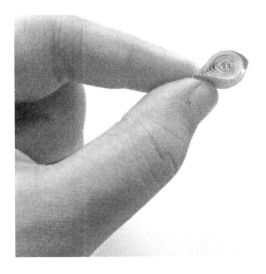

10. Now pinch the opposite side of the strip with the pen to develop another sharp edge. You are now having a shape like teardrop

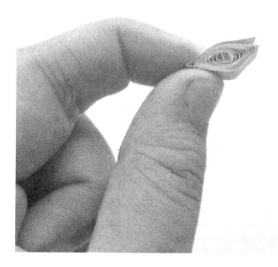

11. Repeat actions 6-10 to develop 5 more teardrop shapes using the identical colored strips for a total of 6. Make 3 more shapes on the third color of the paper

12. **Get a notepad or plastic with a smooth surface** (so you can easily remove the glued pieces). Place the central part of the flower on its surface. Take the first 2 shapes of your color of which you have six and join them in the circle. Do this by gluing any of the pointed edges to the center circle. Also glue the rounded part of the eye shapes together, joining their petals together

13. Now take one of your second color of the shaped swirls and glue it the same way in the center and on the adjacent petal

14. Repeat the pattern until the shape of the paper quilling flower is complete

15. **Develop a narrow coil with a relatively larger ring in the center**

16. **Attach the spiral to the floral pattern between two of your petals to make it circulate.** If you want to print your design, now is the time to do it. Make sure you leave the hole in the coil you made in step 15 open.

17. Place a diving ring through the coil ring to complete the pendant

18. **Attach your jump ring to a cable or chain and wear it with pride.** If you want to add beads, you will need to finish your chain or remove the accompanying endings and choose large beads with holes as accents

Wear it and be proud of your paper flower skills!

How to make a purple quilling paper flower necklace with decorated white pearls

Now let's see how to make the purple quilling paper flower necklace with decorated white pearls.

Materials needed:

- Quilling paper strip set
- 10mm White Round Pearl Beads
- 8mm white round pearl beads
- 6mm white round pearl beads
- Round flat white pearl cabochons
- Iron cross chains
- Silver jump rings
- Silver brooches
- Silver eyepins
- Round magnetic clasps in silver 11.5 x 6 mm
- Needle pliers
- Round nose pliers
- Rotating pen
- Tweezers
- White glue.

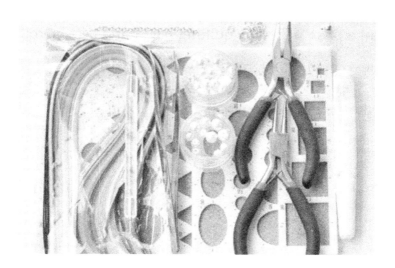

Steps:

1. **Make the first part of the purple quilling paper flower pendant**

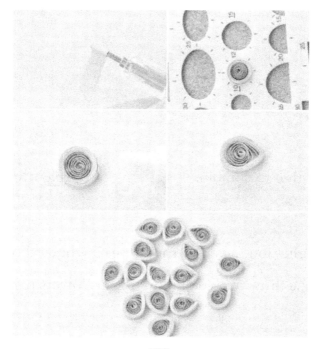

First, cut a piece of purple quilling paper and use the rolling pin to create a circular pattern.

Use white glue to fix the circular pattern and glue the endings.

Transform the circular motif into a teardrop motif.

Use white glue to combine 5 patterns of purple drops into one flower.

Use white glue to glue a flat round pearl white cabochon in the middle of the three purple quilling paper flowers respectively.

2. Make the remaining part of the purple quilling paper flower pendant

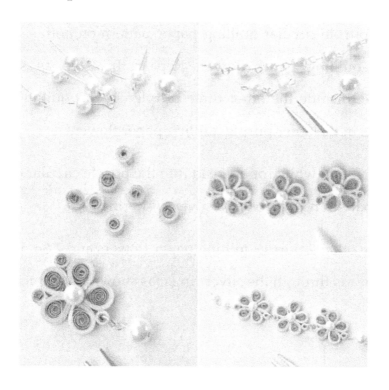

First, it integrates a 10mm white round pearl, 3 8mm white round pearls and 5 6mm white round pearls with the silver clips one by one.

Circle the other end of the silver pins. Combine 3 6mm white round beads with 3 8mm white round beads. Combine two 6mm white round beads together.

Refer to step 1 to make 7 more purple circular quilling paper patterns.

Add a purple circular quilling paper pattern on both sides of a purple quilling paper flower. Repeat this step as soon as possible. Include the other three purple circular quilling paper patterns in the other purple quilling paper flower.

Put the 10mm white round bead into the purple circular quilling paper pattern hole through a silver jump ring.

Add the other 2 purple quilling paper flowers and 2 6mm round white beads through the silver rings (as shown in the picture).

3. Make the rest part of the purple quilling paper flower medallion

Add the 6 white round bead pattern to the hole of the other purple circular pattern through a silver dive ring. Cut 2 pieces of silver braided chain (approximately the same length) and include them on the two sides respectively.

Attach the two ends of the purple quilling paper flower locket via a 11.5 x 6mm silver round magnetic clasp and 2 silver dip rings.

Here is the latest appearance of the purple quilling paper flower necklace.

CHAPTER SIXTEEN

Paper Quilling Snowflakes

Bring the fun of snow into your home with these simple paper snowflake accessories. Feathered snowflakes can vary in style dramatically. Some are extremely comprehensive and remarkable, others are more basic. They can really be done with the more standard quilling shapes.

The tricks are to use proportions in your designs and to keep the shape sizes consistent throughout the snowflake.

Materials:

- A blank sheet of A4 paper (the one you use for printing)
- Fluted quilling tool
- White glue and brush
- Scissors or utility knife
- Pencil
- Rule.

Steps:

1. Make the strips

The first thing to do is divide the sheet of paper into strips.

The strips should be 0.19 inches (0.5 cm) wide and as long as the longest side of the sheet of paper.

It is very important that all the strips are the same width, so use a pencil and a ruler to do this.

When you have finished making all your strips, you should cut them.

Realizing that it would be much faster, I started to cut them with scissors, but after the first strip I used a cutter! Try to be as many as possible in this step.

2. The first reel

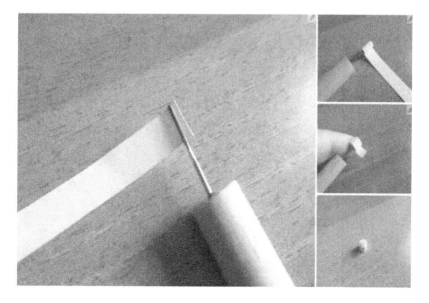

Let's start with the coils!

Take between the strips you just cut and insert between their ends in the quilling tool.

Begin rotating the tool making sure the paper is taut and continue rotating until you reach the other end of the strip.

When you do, remove the paper roll from the tool and tape the end to secure it.

Your first reel is ready!

This will be the center of the snowflake.

3. The tears

Now you need to make another coil like this but before gluing it to close it, release it a little between your fingers so that it is not as tight as the first (loose coil).

Secure it with glue.We will not leave this reel this time.

Press it on one side with your thumb and forefinger to create a teardrop shape. Now do 5 more pieces, for a total of 6.

Glue the tip of the teardrop around the first coil you made, using white glue.

You will get a shape that will remind you of a flower.

4. The eyes

Make 6 loosed coils.

We will provide a new way now. Instead of pressing it only on one side, you need to press the coil with both hands at the same time so that the coil becomes more like an oval. This is called an eye.

Make 6 eyes like this and glue them between the petals of the "flower" you made earlier.

5. Smaller coils

Now cut 3 strips in half to get 6 strips.

With these shorter strips you need to make 6 narrow coils, similar to the first one you made. The only difference is that they will end up being smaller, of course.

6. The first snowflake

Glue the smaller coils to the tips of the "eyes" you made in step 4, always using white glue.

Since these shapes are so small and round, you need to press them down a bit to make sure they stick together.

This is already a good snowflake!

If you want to keep it that way, skip the following steps and go to step 9.

7. More loose coils

Now make 6 regular loose spirals and glue them on the tears, between the eyes.

8. The squares

Let's create a new shape now.

Roll out 6 looser coils and secure with glue.

Shaping them with the fingertips to get a square. You have to press on 2 sides as you did with your eyes, then push the coil in to develop 2 more angles. Rotate it to change it.

Glue the edge of the squares to the large loose coils you created in step 7.

9. **You need a coil with a hole in the center to be able to hang the snowflake**

To do this, use a thin cylinder (I used the handle of my quilling tool, a round pencil would work too) and twist a strip around like you did the other coils. The only difference is that instead of gluing the paper only at the end, I also glued it at the beginning, to make sure that the paper forms a circle that doesn't move inward. Glue this piece to one of the tight coils of your snowflake. You can also apply a little clear varnish over the entire surface to make your design shiny and more durable if you prefer.

String a thread through the hole and you're ready to hang your snowflake on your Christmas tree!

ANOTHER METHOD

Follow our easy instructions to fold and cut paper into distinctive, eye-catching paper snowflakes.

Materials needed:

- Paper (preferably thin or light paper)

- Pair of scissors

- Conveyor *(optional)*.

Steps:

1. **Make a square out of paper**

Start with a square, light, or preferably thin sheet of paper. You can use square origami paper or follow these simple actions to make a square out of any rectangular paper.

2. Fold in half diagonally

3. Fold the square diagonally in half to form a triangle

Fold the resulting triangle in half to make a smaller triangle.

4. Divide the triangle into 3 sections

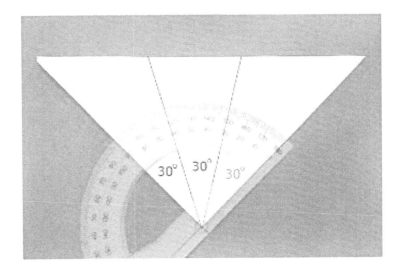

The most crucial and perhaps the most complicated step in creating a paper snowflake is dividing the triangle into three equivalent sections. The most accurate way to do this is to use a protractor to divide the angle at the vertex of the triangle (the angle opposite the longest side) into three areas, each at a 30-degree angle. If you don't have a protractor, you can approximate the size of the areas by following steps 5 and 6.

5. Fold the left section

Fold the left section forward as soon as you have marked the 3 equivalent sections.

6. Fold the right section

Fold the ideal section forward.

7. Rotate the shape

Flip the shape over so the side with the horizontal edge meets the front.

8. Cut along the horizontal edge

Cut along the horizontal edge to make a wedge.

9. Cut out random shapes

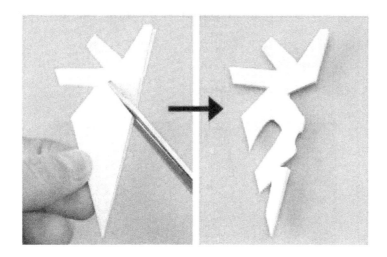

Keeping the wedge bent, cut random shapes from the edges.

If you are looking to find ready-to-cut snowflake patterns, you can find them online.

Open the card

Open the paper completely to reveal your paper snowflake. Like real snowflakes, your paper snowflake has a 6-pointed or 6-sided balance.

10. Create more snowflakes

In nature, no two snowflakes are exactly alike. Try editing the shape cutouts in step 9 to create your own unique snowflakes.

CHAPTER SEVENTEEN

Paper Quilling Watermelon Jewelry

Watermelon pendant

Materials:

- 5mm filigree strips in red, white, light green and dark green or Glue

- Holder for pendants (rings)

- Filigree needle

- Black marker.

How to make your own watermelon pendant with the duvet

Steps:

1. Create a narrow bobbin using 15 strips of red quilling

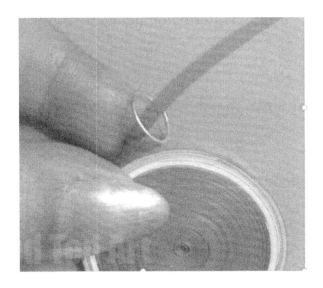

2. **Take 2 strips of white quilling and wrap them around the narrow red bobbin.** Take 2 strips of light green quilling and repeat the same procedure, except on the white color.

3. **Continue the process of the dark green strips to, keep in mind that as you cover it around the light green color, after one round of wrapping, put a pendant to hang across the strip and continue wrapping.** Whenever you reach the pendant holder, pass the quilling strip through it and not over it. As soon as it is complete, glue the end of the paper.

4. With a black marker, draw small dots all over the red spool and voila! Your watermelon feather pendant is ready!

CHAPTER EIGHTEEN

Paper Quilling Frequently Asked Questions

- **What is Quilling?**

Quilling is an ancient art form whose roots are to be discovered in the Middle East, it is probably in Ancient Egypt where we should find its noble origins. It is an art type that involves the use of hand-rolled, shaped and glued strips of paper to develop decorative styles. There are lots of shapes and methods that can be utilized in Quilling art. The most utilized shapes are: the circle, the drop, the eye, the triangle, the square, the leaf, the crescent, the star, the arrow and the tulip. Rather the most used techniques are: Quilling Comb (Comb Technique), Quilling Beheeve (Beehive Technique), Husking Technique, Quilling Edge and quilling comb.

- **What are the creations made of?**

The material mostly used to make such creations is PAPER. When it involves 3D items and bijoux, the paper is treated with non-toxic water-based paint for shock and wetness resistance.

- **What type of card do you use? What is the weight of the quilling paper?**

For my quilling jobs I use a large choice of colored papers and cards. In particular, I use Fabriano, Favini, Canson paper and great papers of different weights. The paper weight differs according to the quilling job I have to make. I use weights from 80 g/ m2, 120 g/ m2 and up to 220 g/ m2 for paper strips.

- **Can I create quilling painting?**

Yup! You have the ability to recreate a quilling painting. However it will not be precisely similar due to the qualities of a handmade craft product, however it will be really comparable.

- **Can I make any type of quilling (paintings, eco-bijoux)?**

Yes sure! I personally make every single creation in quilling. With the help of a quilling pen and other specific tools, I hand roll each private strip of paper, glue it and pattern it to form various shapes that will eventually comprise a genuinely

- **I would like a specific style, can I make it in quilling?**

Naturally! Personalized creations are the ones that excite me most! Gather your idea and develop a custom-made creation for yourself based upon your preferences and requirements. In addition to individualized wedding event favors, You can make the best paintings and squares as a wedding event present, birth gift, anniversary present, birthday present, etc

- **How do I look after my paper quilling jewelry?**

Eco-Bijoux and 3D Objects: these items are protected with water-based paints (non-toxic). Once applied in 2 or 3 layers, the paint will secure the paper, making it resistant to wetness and shocks. To clean a 3D object in Quilling just use a brush with soft bristles. The paint I use (without toxic substances) soaks into the paper, making it stiff, strong and appropriate for daily usage. However it is advised to prevent prolonged contact with water as the paint does not make the paper object completely waterproof. Please do not shower or shower with the jewelry. Just as you would look after any valuable art piece, proper storage of your jewelry and/ or ornaments in a precious jewelry box is recommended and you will extend their life.

• **How do I best protect a painting in Quilling?**

All my paintings are protected by glass or Plexiglas and are intended specifically for indoor environments. They must for that reason be kept in a dry location, safeguarded from heat sources, sources of humidity and direct sunlight.

• **Which frame sizes are suitable for Quilling?**

The size of the frame generally depends upon the quilling design I'm going to make. Given that a quilling work is three-dimensional and has more "height" than pictures or printed works of art, it needs a unique frame, appropriate for consisting of 3d developments. These frames are called "Shadowboxes" (ie deep frames). All frames have a glass or plexiglass security depending on the model selected.

Here are the basic 3D frames you can use:

- Small measurements: external steps 13x18 cm; 19x13 cm
- Typical measurements: external steps 25x25 cm (internal design area: 21x21 cm); 23.7 x23.7 cm (interior design space: 20.5 x20.5); 21x30cm
- Huge size: external measures 30x40 cm (internal style area:-RRB-; 24x43 cm; 30x30 cm.
- Extra big: external dimensions 40x50 cm (internal design space:-RRB-; 40x50 cm; 50x70 cm; 61x91 cm.

- **For how long does it take to develop a custom painting in Quilling?**

Each of the quilling paintings can take from around 4 hours to 20 hours (in some cases a lot more) to make. This depends upon the intricacy and size of the quilling style.

- **Can I make present boxes and customized messages?**

Yes sure! On request, you can get tailored present boxes. I commit a lot of attention and care to the packaging, motivated by the Japanese art of covering "Tsutsumi" according to which, the product packaging is just as important as the present itself, maybe much more.

- **What kind of card should a beginner use?**

Computer printer paper cut into narrow strips (1/8 inch or 3mm) will be fine for practice. When you are ready for real quilling paper, the easiest thing to do is buy it online as you will find a much better selection than in craft stores. The US quilling suppliers are excellent and have American paper brands such as Paplin, Lake City and Quilled Creations, and also the British brand J.J. Quilling designs. The card is pretty cheap, but you may want to join the subscriber list as sales are used occasionally. All are shipped worldwide.

- **I can't understand quilling. How long does it take to learn?**

Because stocks are so simple, quilling is one of those things that people believe should be very easy and straightforward. Roll paper starts to look totally natural after a couple of hours of practice. Not bad for a hobby that could last a lifetime! At first, feeling all the thumbs, I had to keep informing myself that if other people could do it, I could too, it's just paper and glue.

- **Which type of quilling paper works best?**

There are numerous impressive options; solid colors, pearl, metal, parchment, parchment, gold trim and gradient colors are just some of the options. Each type handles slightly differently, but they all roll smoothly. Quilling paper is slightly heavier and softer than computer systems paper. The strips come in various widths ranging from narrow (about 1/16 inch) to 1 inch and most are packaged in multi-colored packaging in addition to individual colors.

- **What quilling tool do you use?**

My favorite tool has an ultra-fine groove, the center crimp sticking out of the groove is barely noticeable. The tool is now available through the Etsy shop.

I use a standard slit tool to make folded roses and when I want coils with round centers without crimping, I use a needle tool. All vendors offer a range of tools; you will surely find one that works for you. Use a stiff wire, my first tool was a muffin tester from my kitchen drawer if you want to get started right away while you wait for your tool to arrive here!

- **What kind of glue do you suggest and how do you apply it?**

My favorite is a clear gel adhesive, as it doesn't create a leathery surface compared to white craft glue. It is odorless and, like quality quilling paper, does not contain acids. My approach to using glue on a reel is to tap on a plastic cap, then pick up an extremely high percentage with the suggestion of a paper piercing tool, cocktail stick, or T-pin. Some prefer to use an ultrafine pointer glue applicator.

• How do you know what size to make loose coils?

I see models that say they use a 3 inch strip wrapped in a loose coil. I have a circular measurement chart, but I don't understand which length strip should go into which hole.

• Are there any standards?

There are no standards. Its three-inch strip can make a slightly different sized coil than another quiller's three-inch strip; it just depends on how hard you roll the paper. The main thing is to roll with tension and your work will have good harmony. The gauge of the rim helps to make the coils of constant size.

• Don't your hands cramp when you put the pen down?

I am happy to say that the answer is no. It can happen if you hold a tool too tightly and / or work for a long time without waiting time. Let's face it, any kind of repeated movement can cause injury. Consciously maintain a relaxed grip on the instrument and periodically extend your hands and fingers. You may want to secure the padding around the tender for maximum comfort. For me it is an enigma why companies do not regularly create all the tools with ergonomically sound management.

- **Where can I buy quilling paper for writing?**

I can't find quilling paper thicker than regular paper.

Real quilling paper is not as heavy as cardstock, which does not normally roll easily. If you are going to make a curved stripe, the border design (like for the letters) tries cheap cardstock - simply put, very thin.

For the letters, I prefer to use 2 strips of quilling paper glued together. Between the double density and the glue, the paper ends up being quite strong, yet it keeps rolling smoothly. Keep a comfortable damp cloth and slide it down both sides of the strip to remove excess glue as soon as you have attached them. Then, set the strip aside and wait for the glue to dry completely before trying to roll it up.

- **What do you use to cover your finished quilling?**

I don't usually use a fixative because I like the natural look of the paper. Some fasteners produce a glossy plastic finish and application can cause the coil centers to swell. The glass protects it if I made a framed piece. BrushableLiquitex varnish is excellent and is offered in gloss or matte if you are concerned about extreme humidity. Apply an extremely fine pair of coats, never excessive at the same time.

- **How is quilling paper saved?**

There are probably as many answers to this question as there are quillers! The main points to remember is to store the strips in a dry, dust-free place and out of direct sunlight. It is helpful to keep the colors labeled by brand / number in the same clear bags that they come in.

- **How do I mail a quilled card?**

Preferably, you would use a sturdy, shallow box lined with bubble wrap. Instead, place your card between two sheets of cardboard and then in an envelope. If you use an air bubbled bulletin board thinking that it provides enough protection, the paper could wrinkle, so I would include a sheet of cardboard under and on top of the ticket. My Quilling Nest offers innovative advertisements for quilling. The marked cardstock folds easily to form a box. I put a layer of bubble wrap on the front of a card as an added defense.

CONCLUSION

If you like making cards and crafts, you would surely love to find great paper quilling ideas that you can use in your productions. You can use them in ornaments, to personalize your gifts, cards and scrapbooks, and many other things you can make with them. When expressing your art you can only limit your creativity.

Of course, in art, it is always great to have your own special style in developing your craft so that you can practice and hone your skills and find new things about it. While this is true, it could also help a lot, particularly in quilling, if you can start with some paper quilling ideas from other people who have learned the trade. From there you can work on your design as fast as you explore many other things you can do with quilling.

In any case, we all have to start with the essentials.

You can select the size of the quilling paper based on the design you need to make. The basic paper size you can use is 1/8 ", which you can cut yourself with a paper cutter or shredder, although you may not get this size in a shredder. If you want them to curl perfectly, buy them. Pre - Cut strips are a great alternative. At least you will get a paper of the same size. If you are just starting out, you may also decide to practice cutting paper yourself to save at least a few dollars while still trying your hand on the plane.

To guide you through the correct size of paper you need, if your quilling work involves fine details, you can request narrower strips of quilling paper, such as 1/16 "in size. For 3D sculpting and fringed designs, it is possible you want to use wider strips - 1/2 "or 1/4". For basic projects or when practicing, 1/8 "would be fine.

You can also choose from a range of colors to enhance the style and concepts of your paper quilling. If you choose your card, be sure to choose something that has the exact same color on the front and back of the card, otherwise it will ruin your surface product. Lightweight cardstock will work just fine.

Glue selection is also important in making your art. Of course, you don't want your pen style to be smeared with visible white glue everywhere. It is recommended that you select a clear dry glue to avoid ruining your art. One method to help you glue your particular creations, including those big curls, is to spread the glue on a piece of paper and with tweezers, you can gently press down on your feathered styles just enough so that the bottom has enough glue. to your album or card. You can also use toothpicks to help it stick.

You can then create your own design and squeeze your innovative juices to create designs that don't exist yet if you master the fundamentals. This will really set your imagination free and allow you to create your own style. If you want to learn more paper quilling ideas and master the art of quilling, you must first figure out how to make standard designs and shapes. You can discover helpful resources that will teach you step-by-step how to transform teardrop styles into square styles and other patterns. In the same way it will work to observe the quilling masters and win with them.

Thank you for reading this book.

If you enjoyed it, please visit the site where you purchased it and write a brief review. Your feedback is important to me and will help other readers decide whether to read the book too.

Thank you!

Brenda Sanders

Made in the USA
Monee, IL
25 October 2024